MW00437343

The Yale
Art + Architecture
Building

The Yale Art + Architecture Building

Photographs by Ezra Stoller

Introduction by Philip Nobel

building blocks

Princeton Architectural Press • New York

The BUILDING BLOCKS series presents the masterworks of modern architecture through the iconic images of acclaimed architectural photographer Ezra Stoller.

Contents

Preface

Ezra Stoller

I MET PAUL RUDOLPH in the late forties when I was rushing around to get photographs of his houses in Sarasota for an *Architectural Forum* story on architects under the age of thirty. Over the fifty years we knew each other, he became a true friend. Paul was a real genius—no question about it. And the longer I knew him, the more impressed I was by his work.

When Paul showed me around the Yale Art and Architecture Building for the first time, he proudly stated that there were over thirty different levels in the building, indicating its great fluidity of space. As I organized my shoot, I chose positions that would capture this aspect of the design.

The building was fully occupied when I photographed it. While not all of the interior spaces had been completed, most of the studios were in use, and this made things tricky. In addition, the exceedingly tight urban spaces and street furniture of New Haven made it difficult to photograph the building's exterior.

In the early 1960s I had just begun working with a 4 x 5 camera—a liberating experience. Previously, I had used an 8 x 10 camera that was heavy and cumbersome. And the film was expensive. Without the freedom and flexibility of the 4 x 5, the sort of coverage produced on this job would not have been possible—a medium-sized project and so many pictures! I did get carried away, but for a good cause.

Changes have since eliminated much of the building's grandeur. Now, I am gratified to know that my photographs are being used as a reference for new renovations more sympathetic to what Paul had originally intended.

Introduction

Philip Nobel

ON THE COVER of its February 1964 issue, *Progressive Architecture* announced the completion of Paul Rudolph's Art and Architecture Building at Yale with a doctored version of an Ezra Stoller photograph. To a raking exterior shot of the building, the magazine's art department added a three-quarters view of Rudolph's face looking down from the facade with characteristic gravity. A close-up of the building's rough "corduroy" concrete, screened across the sky of the photograph, suggested that the architect who had so thoroughly manhandled the environment inside the new school would now take on the world beyond its walls.

Even before the Art and Architecture Building was finished (it was open and substantially complete in the fall of 1963 and dedicated on 9 November of that year), Rudolph's work was often perceived as an aggressive extension of his personality. In the 1961 issue of *Perspecta*, the occasional journal of Yale's architecture school, Walter McQuade wrote that he found Rudolph "disquieting...because he has inserted himself so ruthlessly into his work, has been so recognizable in it. No matter how he varies the recipes for facades, I can see the faultless young crew cut head peering out the windows." McQuade went on to warn that Rudolph would "destroy himself" or "go bad" if he did not reinforce the boundary between his ego and his art—a trick that Rudolph, who died of lung cancer in August 1997, could never learn.[1] (Three months after his death, in a postmortem almost too perfect for nonfiction, 8 ounces of Rudolph's cremated remains were scattered throughout the Art and Architecture Building by Mark Bain, an installation artist who wanted to dust the interior of the building with a "symbolic residue" of its architect.)[2]

WHEN EZRA STOLLER arrived in New Haven to photograph the building on 16 October 1963, he found it in a pristine state that would last for only six years. Famously, on the night of 14 June 1969, the building was damaged severely by a fire of suspicious origin. It suffered further afterwards from a series of unsympathetic renovations that erased many of the spaces that Stoller had photographed and that Rudolph had so lovingly appointed with bizarre archeological artifacts, cargo-netting window shades, and orange pile rugs. After the fire, rooms were closed, merged, or carved out of once open studio spaces; the narrow U-channel concrete bridge that starred in several of Stoller's shots was removed when the gap it spanned was filled-in to squeeze more floor space out of the increasingly compromised building. Not surprisingly, Rudolph came to disown the project entirely. After a lecture in 1993, he refused to answer a question about the building, stating flatly that it "no longer exists for me."[3] Although the suspected fire-bombing of the building was most likely a political rather than an architectural critique, the act has always been interpreted as the ultimate result of a simmering dissatisfaction with the perceived oppressiveness of Rudolph's design. As Vincent

Rudolph's cult of personality gradually eroded following the infamous fire of 14 *June* 1969.

Scully noted in the catalog to an exhibition that coincided with the opening of the building, Rudolph's emphatic, vertiginous space-making and his tendency toward sculptural masses and labyrinthine passages "puts demands upon the individual user that not every psyche will be able to meet."[4]

Paul Rudolph's early career was bracketed by his graduation from Walter Gropius's master-class at Harvard in 1947 and his appointment as the chairman of the Yale Department of Architecture in the fall of 1957. Rudolph was thus at the center of his generation's development for more than a decade, from the very source of its inspiration as a Gropius insider, to the focal point for reaction against that legacy at Yale around 1960. In addition to the favorable reception of his first projects—he was celebrated for the inventive houses he built in Florida in the 1950s—and his reputation as an expert and fanatical draftsman, an important factor in Rudolph's rise to prominence was his knack for playing the role of the maverick; he created a public persona for himself that hovered somewhere between the mysticism of Louis Kahn and Philip Johnson's brashness. This intentionally roguish image made Rudolph a popular and convenient representative for the younger architects who emerged from the schools and the armed services in the years after World War II. Speaking in this capacity at the 1954 convention of the American Institute of Architects, he presented what amounted to a declaration of the principles that were then guiding him and his peers toward sensual alternatives to the universal space of orthodox modernism, ideas that would eventually find form in the Art and Architecture Building:

> We desperately need to relearn the art of disposing buildings to create
> different kinds of space: the quiet, enclosed, shaded space; the hustling
> bustling space pungent with vitality; the paved, dignified, vast, sumptu-

ous, even awe-inspiring space; the mysterious space....We need sequences of spaces which arouse one's curiosity, give a sense of anticipation, which beckon and impel us to rush forward to find that releasing space which dominates, which climaxes and acts as a magnet and gives direction.[5]

Four years later, and several months into his administration at Yale, Rudolph elaborated on this view during his Alumni Day speech, essentially mandating increased expressionism as a means to re-establish the lost grandeur of architecture, and by association its practitioners: "Last on our list [of educational goals at Yale] will be a renewed concern with visual delight. This is indeed the architect's responsibility, for other specialists can do everything else that he does and, quite often, much better."[6] Through statements such as these, and the unrelenting evidence of his designs, Rudolph ultimately became the most celebrated American champion of the strain of post-functionalist architecture widely known as Brutalism.

Rudolph's fall from grace started with his embrace of this mode in the Art and Architecture Building. Begun shortly after his arrival at the school, the building became a sensation. It was widely published—sometimes in tandem with Gordon Bunshaft's jewel box Beinecke Library, completed across campus at the same time—and it was overrun with visitors. In a 1973 interview, Rudolph argued that his building was misunderstood from the start because of this media-bred onslaught: "When it first opened there were literally thousands of people who came to see it, but it was never intended for that. It was intended for a few students who presumably soon learn the purposely secret circulation system."[7] Henry Millon wrote presciently about the potential consequences of this sort of self-indulgent master-building in "Rudolph at the Crossroads," an article in the December 1960 issue of *Architectural Design*: "There is no absolute way to know if Paul

Rudolph is a man of great genius, a better-than-mediocre figure, or, perhaps, a charlatan. But it seems to be clear that he is entering upon a profoundly different phase of his career that might be a more mature phase or might, equally, signal his collapse as a notable figure."[8] The events at the Art and Architecture Building, and the sweeping rejection of monumentality that was architecture's homegrown contribution to the activism of the late 1960s and 1970s, did in the end eclipse Rudolph's career. Although his reputation was revived several times—first by Michael Sorkin and others in the late 1980s, as an antidote to postmodern banality, and later, in his final years, to celebrate him as a surviving modern master—Rudolph never regained the following, as an architect or a teacher, that he enjoyed before the fire.

The form of the Art and Architecture Building—and of the designs it spawned, notably Rudolph's never-completed Boston Government Service Center (1962–72), an equally enthralling and tragic building—owes a lot to the heavily pro-monumental milieu that Rudolph was immersed in at Yale. From the mid-1950s through the end of his term as chairman there a decade later, Yale's architecture school was a crucible for the investigation of alternatives to the expressive limitations of Harvard functionalism. Between 1957 and 1960, for instance, *Perspecta* published early manifestations of interest in primitive architecture, rediscoveries of Antoni Gaudí's Casa Milà and Erich Mendelsohn's sketches, articles on ornament and its proper use, and several appreciations of ruined monuments such as Hadrian's Villa and Macchu Picchu. Sowing reaction to the sterility of mainstream midcentury American architecture, the journal promoted formal and material exploration, the inclusion of history, and heterodoxy over dogma. It also frequently published the work of like-minded architects, some of whom—including Louis Kahn, Eero Saarinen, Marcel Breuer, and Paul Rudolph—were also invited to design buildings for the expanding New Haven campus.

Rudolph at the Art and Architecture Building in 1963.

At Yale, Rudolph was particularly receptive to the ideas of Vincent Scully, the school's popular and influential theorist and professor of architectural history. When Rudolph arrived on campus in 1957, he was already drifting away from the distantly Miesian structural experimentation of his early work. Contact with Scully, an infamous charismatic, reinforced this shift. Scully's thinking from that time is preserved in his book *Modern Architecture*, first published in 1961 but based on a lecture given in 1957 and subsequent articles in *Perspecta* and other journals. As a "way out of academicism for the younger men" and a means to achieve "an architecture reinvested with the tenaciously physical force of Western tradition," Scully championed Le Corbusier's late work, particularly the High Court (1951–56) and other buildings at the government complex in Chandigarh, India.[9] The influence of Le Corbusier, though synthesized, as always, within Rudolph's strong personal vision, was already apparent in the rhythmic sunshades and bold piers of Sarasota High School (1958–62), his first major work after becoming chairman of the architecture school. In Rudolph's words: "Sarasota High School was a move from clear form, from clear structure....It depends much more on the space and the handling of light....But let's face it. All this comes from Corbusier. He, of course, did it all much earlier and much better."[10] The earliest design renderings of the Art and Architecture Building—a commission Rudolph first suggested be offered to Le Corbusier—show a reconfiguration of the planar language he developed at Sarasota, grafted on to an adaptation of the atrium and massing of Frank Lloyd Wright's Larkin Building (1904–5). The more "tenaciously physical" final design that followed was developed only after Rudolph visited Chandigarh in May 1960.

As he designed the Art and Architecture Building, Rudolph was also working on the Temple Street Garage in New Haven (1959–63), which would become an important source for the geometries and

Temple Street Garage, New Haven, 1959–63. *Rudolph animated the concrete surfaces of the garage with imprints of the wood formwork used to construct the building. The dramatically raking light of Stoller's photographs literally highlighted this aspect of Rudolph's design.*

moods of his later buildings. The garage was a testing ground for concrete aesthetics; there, for the first time, Rudolph used board forms in the manner of Le Corbusier to produce various textures, principally flat surfaces marked by low, thin ridges. The important jump from this simple expression of process to the contrivance of Rudolph's signature bush-hammered concrete soon followed in the construction of the Art and Architecture Building. Curiously, the jagged, ridged treatment that may be Rudolph's best-known contribution to his art did not evolve solely from a sculptural urge; it was in part a by-product of his rendering technique. In an essay titled "From Conception to Sketch to Rendering to Building," Rudolph explained this development:

Some construction materials are easier to depict through rendering than are others. This probably accounts for some of my interest in concrete and highly textured surfaces in general. The technique of rendering with line to create light and shadow suggests a certain linearity in the texture of walls which sometimes influences the choice of materials. For instance, the development of textured concrete, as used in many of our buildings, probably started…with the concept of rendering and how to make buildings conform more exactly to the image depicted.[11]

Rudolph's deep involvement with drawing was also forcefully stated in the final cadence of his 1958 Alumni Day address at Yale. There, Rudolph implored the students to be aware of the "exhilarating, awesome moment" at the beginning of a drawing: "When [the architect] takes pencil in hand, and holds it poised above a white sheet of paper, he has suspended there all that has gone before and all that will ever be."[12] This obsession with images belies the brooding heft of Rudolph's buildings; at one level, the brutal concrete is revealed to be a sort of ornamental coating. Rudolph's fascination with "visual delight" also begs a fresh look at the Art and Architecture Building's reputation for bunker crudity. In its original state, the building was, if not exactly playful, at least more humane. In Stoller's photographs, one can find a glimmer of this lost sensitivity in the upper-floor sculpture court or the inscribed mural, like a drunken topographic map, which did not survive the building's travails. At a level of detail too fine for the camera, and in locations too dark for gripping photography, Rudolph indulged his often suppressed sense of whimsy by inserting follies into the concrete itself. In November 1963, *Time* ran an article in which Rudolph—"Yale's 45-year-old architectural Wunderkind"—was portrayed "puckishly" pointing out the nautilus shells and other winking inspirations buried in the walls of the building.[13] With the classical fragments and the adopted Louis

Sullivan ornament, these "conceits," as Rudolph called them, point to a new way to appreciate this complex and very personal building.

One unlikely guide to understanding the Art and Architecture Building is Susan Sontag's 1964 essay "Notes on 'Camp'," in which she describes a detached aestheticism that transcends the banality of earnest criticism—a sort of foppish revelry in the mediocre. "Behind the 'straight' public sense in which something can be taken," she wrote, "one has found a private, zany experience of the thing," as Rudolph did in his play of hidden delights, and as a visitor might when approaching the Art and Architecture Building today.[14] As early as 1973, Charles Jencks made this connection. In his *Modern Movements in Architecture*, Jencks used part of Sontag's definition of camp—that it is a preoccupation with artifice, exaggeration, decoration, and surface at the expense of content (or, in architecture, function)—to place Rudolph among a loose group of "camp" architects that also included Eero Saarinen, Bruce Goff and Minoru Yamasaki.[15] But by deploying Sontag's argument polemically—his camp rubric was little more than a convenient critic's pigeonhole—he overlooked many of the essay's nuances, including one that is particularly relevant today, thirty-five years after the completion of the Art and Architecture Building. In explaining her own attraction to and repulsion from camp artifacts, Sontag wrote that they can be best appreciated when

> the process of aging or deterioration provides the necessary detachment—arouses a necessary sympathy. When the theme is important, and contemporary, the failure of a work of art may make us indignant. Time can change that. Time liberates the work of art from moral relevance, delivering it over to the Camp sensibility.[16]

With Paul Rudolph's death and a new regime at Yale's architecture school pressing to restore its home, the Art and Architecture

Building may be delivered at last. Removed from the debates over its aberrant form, the enmity that may have fueled its disfiguring fire, and even the difficulty of inhabiting the building itself, Rudolph's troubled pile in New Haven can be seen again as he intended it: a playground of epic volumes and a catalog of architectural possibilities weighted heavily toward the grim. The building is a guilty pleasure. It's dank and it's mean and it doesn't work very well—but, oh, what wonderful gloom. As Stoller's photographs attest, and as the building still affirms, few twentieth-century American architects have equaled the dark, visceral joys of the spaces that Paul Rudolph conjured in the Art and Architecture Building, his glory and his greatest regret.

Rudolph on the roof of the Temple Street Garage in 1963.

NOTES

1. Walter McQuade, "The Exploded Landscape," *Perspecta* 7 (1961): 83.

2. Mark Bain, telephone interview with the author, 2 January 1998.

3. Paul Rudolph, lecture at the National Institute for Architectural Education, New York, 2 December 1993.

4. Vincent Scully, "A Note on the Work of Paul Rudolph," unpaginated catalog to the exhibition *The Work of Paul Rudolph, Architect*, Yale University, New Haven, 9 November 1963–6 January 1964.

5. Quoted in "The Changing Philosophy of Architecture," *Architectural Record* (August 1954): 181.

6. Paul Rudolph, "Alumni Day Speech: Yale School of Architecture, February 1958," in *Oppositions* 4 (October 1974): 141–3.

7. John Cook and Heinrich Klotz, *Conversations with Architects* (New York: Praeger, 1973), 98.

8. Henry A. Millon, "Rudolph at the Crossroads," *Architectural Design* (December 1960): 498.

9. Vincent Scully, *Modern Architecture* (New York: Braziller, 1965), 44.

10. Cook and Klotz, *Conversations with Architects*, 95.

11. Yukio Futagawa, ed., *Paul Rudolph: Drawings* (Tokyo: ADA Edita, 1972), 7.

12. Rudolph, "Alumni Day Speech," 143.

13. "New Architecture at Yale," *Time*, 15 November 1963, 85.

14. Susan Sontag, "Notes on 'Camp'," in *Against Interpretation* (New York: Dell Publishing, 1969), 283.

15. Charles Jencks, *Modern Movements in Architecture* (New York: Anchor Books, 1973), ch. 6.

16. Sontag, "Notes on 'Camp'," 286.

Plates

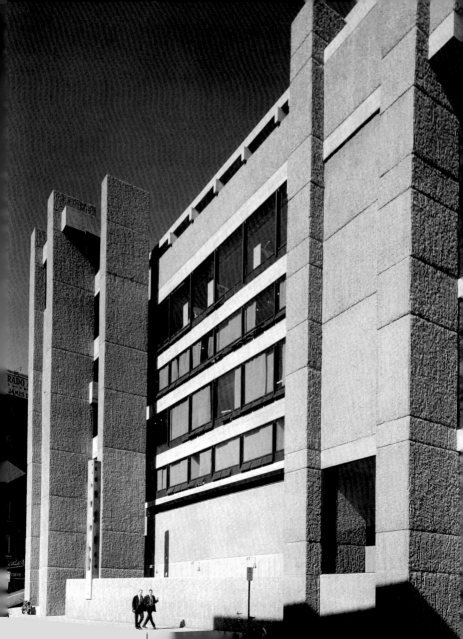

Drawings & Plans

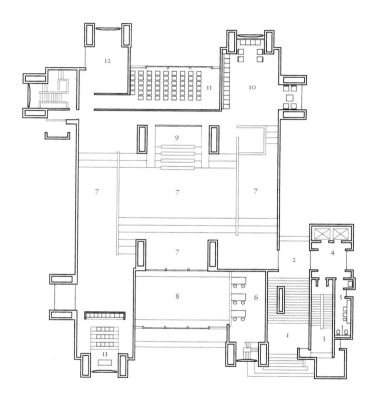

1. STAIRS TO ENTRY   5. BATHROOM   9. JURY

2. LOBBY   6. LIBRARY MEZZANINE   10. STUDENT LOUNGE

3. STAIRWELL   7. EXHIBITION SPACE   11. CLASSROOM

4. ELEVATORS   8. WELL TO LIBRARY   12. RECEIVING

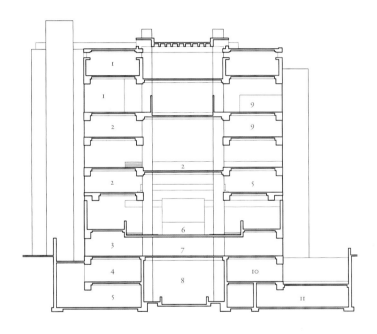

I. PAINTING	4. BASIC DESIGN	8. LECTURE HALL
2. ARCHITECTURAL	5. SCULPTURE	9. URBAN PLANNING
STUDIOS	6. EXHIBITION SPACE	10. GRAPHICS
3. STUDY	7. LIBRARY	11. DRAFTING

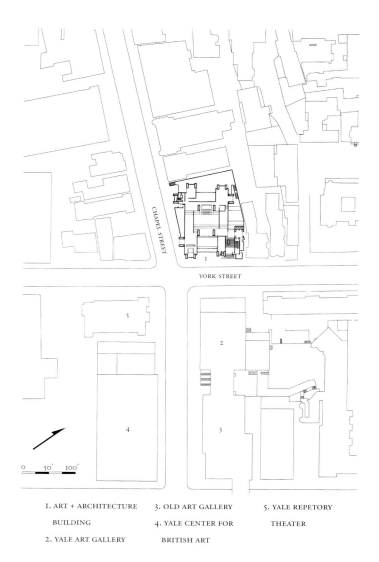

CHAPEL STREET

YORK STREET

1. ART + ARCHITECTURE
BUILDING

2. YALE ART GALLERY

3. OLD ART GALLERY

4. YALE CENTER FOR
BRITISH ART

5. YALE REPETORY
THEATER

0   50'   100'

Key to Photographs

[*] *All photographs taken by Ezra Stoller in 1963.*

Published by
Princeton Architectural Press
37 East Seventh Street
New York, NY 10003

For a catalog of books published by Princeton Architectural Press, call toll free 800.722.6657
or visit www.papress.com

Copyright © 1999 Princeton Architectural Press
All photographs copyright © Esto Photographics, Inc.
03 02 01 00 99   5 4 3 2 1   First Edition

No part of this book may be used or reproduced in any manner without
written permission from the publisher except in the context of reviews.

Editor & book design: Mark Lamster
Drawings: Jonah Pregerson & Mark Watanabe

Acknowledgments: I would like to thank my colleagues at Esto Photographics, especially
Kent Draper and Laura Bolli; Mary Doyle and Mike Kimines of TSI for their help in
preparing these images; and Mark Lamster for his support from start to finish—Erica Stoller

Princeton Architectural Press acknowledges Eugenia Bell, Bernd-Christian Döll, Jane
Garvie, Caroline Green, Leslie Ann Kent, Clare Jacobson, Therese Kelly, Annie Nitschke,
and Sara E. Stemen—Kevin C. Lippert, publisher

For the licensing of Ezra Stoller images, contact Esto Photographics.
Fine art reproductions of Stoller prints are available through the James Danziger Gallery.

Printed in China

Library of Congress Cataloging-in-Publication Data
The Yale Art and Architecture Building / photographs by Ezra Stoller ;
  introduction by Philip Nobel. -- 1st ed.
      p.   cm. -- (The Building Blocks series)
  Includes bibliographical references.
  ISBN 1-56898-185-6 (alk. paper)
  1. Yale University, School of Art and Architecture--Buildings--
Pictorial works. 2. New Haven (Conn.)--Buildings, structures, etc.
--Pictorial works. 3. Rudolph, Paul, 1918–1997--Criticism and
interpretation.   I. Stoller, Ezra. II. Title: Yale Art Architecture Building.
III. Series: Building blocks series (New York, N.Y.)
NA2300.Y36Y37   1999
779'.47468--dc21   98-52455
                                                  CIP